The British Museum

MUSEUMS OF THE WORLD

By Jennifer Howse

www.av2books.com

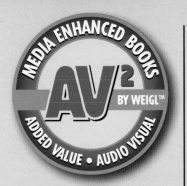

BOOK CODE

A486955

Go to **www.av2books.com**, and enter this book's unique code.

AV² by Weigl brings you media enhanced books that support active learning.

AV² provides enriched content that supplements and complements this book. Weigl's AV² books strive to create inspired learning and engage young minds in a total learning experience.

Your AV² Media Enhanced books come alive with...

Audio
Listen to sections of the book read aloud.

Key Words
Study vocabulary, and complete a matching word activity.

Video
Watch informative video clips.

Quizzes
Test your knowledge.

Embedded Weblinks
Gain additional information for research.

Slide Show
View images and captions, and prepare a presentation.

Try This!
Complete activities and hands-on experiments.

... and much, much more!

Published by AV² by Weigl
350 5th Avenue, 59th Floor
New York, NY 10118
Websites: www.av2books.com   www.weigl.com

Library of Congress Cataloging-in-Publication Data
Howse, Jennifer.
The British Museum / Jennifer Howse.
   pages cm. — (Museums of the world)
Includes index.
ISBN 978-1-4896-1186-4 (hardcover : alk. paper)
ISBN 978-1-4896-1187-1 (softcover : alk. paper)
ISBN 978-1-4896-1188-8 (single user ebk.) — ISBN 978-1-4896-1189-5 (multi user ebk.)
1. British Museum—History--Juvenile literature. I. Title.
  AM101.L62H69 2014
  069.09421--dc23

          2014006381

Printed in North Mankato, Minnesota, in the United States of America
1 2 3 4 5 6 7 8 9 0   18 17 16 15 14

042014
WEP150314

Editor: Heather Kissock
Design: Dean Pickup

Every reasonable effort has been made to trace ownership and to obtain permission to reprint copyright material. The publishers would be pleased to have any errors or omissions brought to their attention so that they may be corrected in subsequent printings.

Weigl acknowledges Getty Images, Alamy, and Newscom as its primary image suppliers for this title.

Contents

What Is the British Museum?

The British Museum, in London, England, is a place to explore and understand many **cultures**. The museum's galleries showcase the shared expressions of people from all parts of the world, indicating how they lived and changed over the years. The **exhibits** in the British Museum are the result of centuries of work. British explorers spanned the globe and collected objects and cultural symbols. The British Museum is one of the world's greatest museums because of their travels.

The British Museum's **collection** contains more than eight million **artifacts**. This massive collection represents time periods from two million years ago to the present day. The museum complex features 100 exhibit rooms, which cover about 800,000 square feet (74,000 square meters) of floor space. However, as large as this may seem, only one percent of the British Museum's collection can be on display at any given time.

1st

The British Museum was the
world's first national public museum.

At least
6 million people
visit the British Museum every year.

FREE

Admission to the British Museum is FREE.

The British Museum complex is about the size of
9 soccer fields.

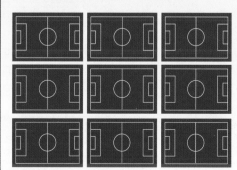

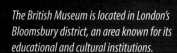
The British Museum is located in London's Bloomsbury district, an area known for its educational and cultural institutions.

History of the British Museum

The British Museum came to be as the result of a will. Sir Hans Sloane, a London doctor, agreed to leave his private collection to the government in exchange for £20,000. The government quickly accepted this arrangement and held a public lottery to raise the money. The proceeds were then used to make the purchase and establish the museum. The British Museum was incorporated in 1753, and a group of **trustees** were charged with planning the museum. After much discussion, they decided to grant free admission to all "studious and curious persons."

The Sloane Collection included a variety of items, ranging from plants to turban buttons.

1759 The British Museum opens to the public on January 15.

1823 To accommodate a growing collection, construction begins on a new building for the British Museum.

1750　　　　**1800**　　　　**1850**

1827 The King's Library becomes the first part of the new building to be completed.

1857 The new British Museum, which forms the core of today's building, completes construction.

In its early days, the British Museum was housed in a private home. Montagu House, a mansion in the Bloomsbury district, was bought for £10,000.

1880s The natural history collections, which include plant and animal **specimens**, are moved to a new building, creating the city's Natural History Museum.

1931 The construction of the Duveen Gallery begins. This gallery is built to display sculptures from the Parthenon, in Greece.

2003 The British Museum celebrates its 250th anniversary.

1900

1950

2000

1907 The foundation stone is laid for the King Edward VII galleries. They open in 1914.

1973 The museum's library collections become part of the British Library. However, the materials are not moved to their new building until 1997.

2000 Queen Elizabeth II opens the Great Court. This enclosed area replaces the former library and houses the Reading Room and an education center.

Key People

By donating his private collection to the British Museum, Hans Sloane became the museum's founder. His donation was, however, only the first. In the years that followed, the British Museum began receiving more donations from private collectors, royalty, and even museum staff. The museum's collection grew as a result of these **benefactors**.

Sir Hans Sloane (1660–1753)

Hans Sloane was Irish by birth. However, his early interest in natural history led him to study medicine in England and France. By 1689, he had a successful medical practice in London, which attracted a number of high-profile clients. The success of his medical career allowed him to indulge in his passion for collecting. He traveled as far away as Jamaica to acquire plant species and live specimens. Sloane also acquired items from other collectors. By the time of his death, at the age of 93, his collection consisted of more than 71,000 objects, including natural history specimens, **antiquities**, books, and coins.

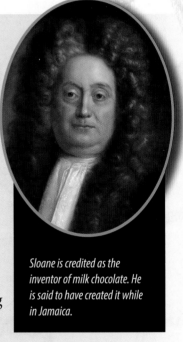

Sloane is credited as the inventor of milk chocolate. He is said to have created it while in Jamaica.

Charles Townley (1737–1805)

A wealthy **patron** of the arts, Charles Townley was a member of the **Royal Society** and a trustee of the British Museum. He was also a collector of Greek and Roman antiquities. As a child, Townley was educated in France. After finishing his formal schooling, he embarked on the **Grand Tour**. During three separate trips through Italy and Greece, Townley purchased numerous artworks and antiquities. His travels created an incredible collection, which, upon Townley's death, was sold to the British Museum for £20,000.

Townley's marbles became the foundation for the British Museum's Greco-Roman galleries.

Sir Joseph Banks (1743–1820)

Born into a wealthy London family, Joseph Banks showed a keen interest in natural history from an early age. Educated at Oxford University, he later began a career as an explorer and **botanist**. His travels took him to North America, the South Pacific, and South America. Everywhere he went, Joseph Banks collected plant and animal specimens, as well as cultural artifacts from the different peoples he encountered. In 1778, he donated his entire **ethnographic** collection to the British Museum. That same year, he was elected president of the Royal Society. This post also made him a trustee of the British Museum.

In 1768, Banks joined a Royal Society expedition that went to explore the South Pacific. He later had a group of islands in the region named after him.

Sir Augustus Wollaston Franks (1826–1897)

Augustus Wollaston Franks is best known for his **curatorial** contributions to the British Museum. His early years were spent in continental Europe, where he received much of his education. Franks returned to England to attend Cambridge University, graduating with a Master of Arts degree in 1852. By that time, he had already begun working at the British Museum as an assistant in the antiquities department. His knowledge of antiquities brought him much recognition. In 1866, he was named the museum's first curator of British and **medieval** antiquities. As curator, Franks managed the existing collection and acquired new pieces. Some of the pieces he obtained for the museum were donated from his personal collection.

Franks gave the British Museum more than 3,000 items from his personal collection.

The British Museum Today

The British Museum has grown substantially from its early days. Its millions of artifacts are now distributed among 10 curatorial departments. Each of these departments has its own collection, research center, and library. To accommodate these collections and expand into new areas, the museum has taken steps to use its space effectively. The creation of the Queen Elizabeth II Great Court was the beginning of a new era in the museum's development. Since then, the museum has restored its oldest room, the King's Library, and established new permanent galleries for Chinese ceramics, timepieces, artifacts from medieval Europe, and an Egyptian tomb-chapel. These developments have helped the British Museum increase its attendance. In 2013, a record 6.7 million visitors came through the doors.

The Queen Elizabeth II Great Court is the largest covered public space in Europe. The museum's reading room is the centerpiece of the court.

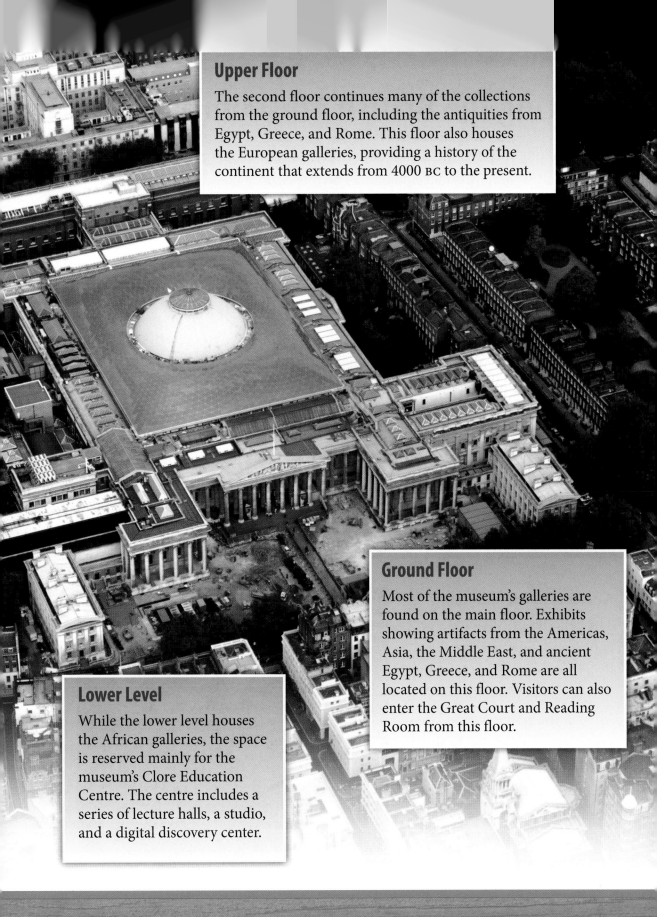

Upper Floor

The second floor continues many of the collections from the ground floor, including the antiquities from Egypt, Greece, and Rome. This floor also houses the European galleries, providing a history of the continent that extends from 4000 BC to the present.

Ground Floor

Most of the museum's galleries are found on the main floor. Exhibits showing artifacts from the Americas, Asia, the Middle East, and ancient Egypt, Greece, and Rome are all located on this floor. Visitors can also enter the Great Court and Reading Room from this floor.

Lower Level

While the lower level houses the African galleries, the space is reserved mainly for the museum's Clore Education Centre. The centre includes a series of lecture halls, a studio, and a digital discovery center.

Touring the British Museum

To walk through the British Museum is to take a journey through the course of human development. The museum's galleries tell the stories of people from all ages and from around the world. The depth of the collection is such that it covers two million years of human history.

Along with mummies, the mummy exhibit at the British Museum features coffins, death masks, and other artifacts related to burial rites of ancient Egyptians.

Ancient Egyptian Galleries

Visitors to the Ancient Egyptian galleries have an opportunity to view the art and artifacts of people who lived along the Nile River thousands of years ago. Everyday objects, such as furniture, are on display, as well as sculptures and jewelry. Many people come to see the mummy collection. Besides humans, the collection also includes mummies of cats.

Ancient Greece and Rome

The galleries of Ancient Greece and Rome showcase the different cultures that have lived in these lands over the years. Most of the artifacts found here were part of archaeological digs in the 18th and 19th centuries. They include marble and bronze sculptures, pottery, coins, and metalwork.

The Parthenon sculptures became part of the British Museum's collection in 1816. They are considered to be a key part of the museum's collection.

European Galleries Artifacts in these galleries show how European society evolved from 10,000 BC to the present. Exhibits display the farming tools of early residents and machines created during the **Industrial Revolution**. Other galleries show the cultural impact that other countries have had on Europe.

The Sutton Hoo ship burial exhibit gives visitors to the museum a glimpse into life in 7th-century Europe.

Galleries of the Americas These galleries focus mainly on the **indigenous** peoples of the Americas. Exhibits include historic artifacts as well as contemporary artworks. The effect of European settlement on these peoples is also explored.

American Indian totem poles are just one type of artifact found in the British Museum's Americas galleries.

One of the European galleries is devoted entirely to **clocks and watches.**

The sculpture of Egyptian ruler Ramesses II **weighs 8 tons** (7.26 metric tons). This is only a fragment of the original statue.

The British Museum has **194 storerooms** on site for artifacts not on display.

Buckingham Palace almost became the home of the British Museum.

During World War II, some of the Parthenon sculptures were stored in London's subway.

22 years

The amount of time it took experts to crack the code on the Rosetta stone

The Lewis chessmen were found buried in a sand dune on Scotland's Isle of Lewis.

The Easter Island moai originally stood on top of a

985-foot cliff. (300-m)

The mask of Quetzalcoatl is carved from a

a single piece of cedar wood.

1.8 million years

The estimated age of the Olduvai stone chopping tool, the museum's oldest artifact

Treasures of the British Museum

When acquiring artifacts, the British Museum's emphasis is on finding works that are historically important. Some of the artifacts, such as statues and monuments, are symbolic. They represent the ideas or beliefs of a cultural group. Others show the reality of life at a certain time and place. They indicate how people found food, where they slept, and what they did for fun. The British Museum is careful in choosing its artifacts. It wants to be certain that these artifacts reflect history accurately.

The scope of the British Museum's collection allows visitors to compare how different cultural groups approached aspects of life. For instance, several galleries feature artifacts relating to war and warriors, including the samurai of Japan.

Lewis Chessmen Carved from walrus ivory and whales' teeth, this chess set is believed to have been created in Norway around 1200 AD. Each piece reflects an aspect of Norse culture. The rooks, for instance, are fashioned after mythical warriors called berserkers.

The Lewis chessmen were found in Scotland in the 1800s.

The text on the Rosetta stone pays tribute to Ptolemy V and all the good he did for the people of Egypt.

Rosetta Stone This granite stone helped archaeologists unlock the ancient Egyptian form of writing called hieroglyphics. Dated to 196 BC, the stone was found near Rosetta, Egypt, in 1799. The message on the stone was written in three ways. Besides hieroglyphics, it contained text in Egyptian and Greek. Experts were able to use their knowledge of these languages to translate the hieroglyphics.

Mosaic Mask of Quetzalcoatl According to Aztec myth, Quetzalcoatl was a feathered serpent and the god of death and rebirth. The mask was made in the 15th or 16th century. Covered with squares of turquoise stones, it was probably worn by Aztec leaders during ceremonies.

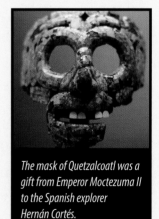

The mask of Quetzalcoatl was a gift from Emperor Moctezuma II to the Spanish explorer Hernán Cortés.

The Easter Island moai was originally red and white. The colors wore off when the statue was transferred from the island to the ship.

Easter Island Statue Strange and foreboding, the statue, or *moai*, was **excavated** from Orongo, Easter Island. It is a rare artifact from the cultures of the South Pacific Islands. Carved from gray basalt, the statue has a height of 2.65 yards (2.42 m) and weighs about 4.6 tons (4.2 metric tons). Created by the Rapa Nui people, it is believed to pay tribute to their ancestors.

Collection Conservation

The artifacts at the British Museum require special care to ensure that they remain unchanged for as long as possible. A team of museum workers called **conservators** have the huge task of caring for all eight million objects in the collection. The conservation lab at the British Museum is a place where conservators use scientific methods to ensure artifacts are stored, cleaned, repaired, and displayed in the best conditions. The techniques used there are similar to those used in museums around the world.

Storage Storing an artifact securely is the best way to prevent damage. Conservators often make cases, or forms, that are designed to fit an artifact's exact shape. This allows every piece of the artifact to be protected and supported. Forms are especially useful with human-shaped statues. Arms and fingers rest inside grooves designed specifically for them, so they remain secure if jostled when moving.

Museums often store small artifacts in drawer cabinets.

Cleaning Dirt and bacteria can break down the fibers of a material, causing it to deteriorate over time. Conservators ensure that artifacts are cleaned regularly. Different cleaning techniques are used depending on the material being cleaned. Small vacuums allow dust to be removed from feathers. Water can be used to clean certain textiles. Some artifacts require special **solvents**. The substances in these liquids and gels help dissolve the buildup of grime.

Brushes and vacuums are often used together. The brushes loosen the dust and grime, and the vacuum picks them up.

After working on an artifact, conservators create condition reports which detail the steps they have taken to conserve it. These reports help other conservators understand the history of the object and how to best conserve it for the future.

Pest Control Insects and other pests can enter a museum in a number of ways. They can be brought into the museum in food products or on clothing. An artifact can be infested before it is even acquired by the museum. Pests can eat through materials and cause permanent damage. Some techniques used to get rid of insects include setting sticky traps and changing the temperature of the room where the pests have been found.

Wood is especially vulnerable to insect infestations.

Climatic Conditions Temperature, **humidity**, and light can damage artifacts. These conditions are often controlled by placing an artifact inside a sealed display case. Monitors placed inside the case provide readings on humidity levels around the artifact, as well as the temperature and amount of light to which the artifact is exposed. By taking these steps, conservators preserve the condition of the artifact so that it can be enjoyed and studied for many years.

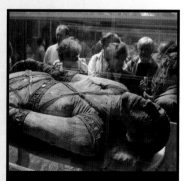

Some artifacts, such as mummies, are very climate sensitive and may decompose if conditions are not maintained.

The British Museum in the World

The purpose of any museum is to hold artifacts, artworks, and even ideas in the public trust. The job of the British Museum's curators, librarians, and educators is to help visitors understand the importance of the artifacts in its collection. Museum staff also reach outside the building to teach people in other parts of the world about these artifacts and what they represent.

Traveling Exhibits Every year, the British Museum organizes exhibits that are sent to other museums around the world. These exhibits give the British Museum the opportunity to share parts of its collection with people who cannot visit the museum itself. The artifacts in the exhibit often have a theme, whether it is the exploration of a time or a specific cultural group. This allows people to understand the artifacts in a specific **context**.

Online Community The internet allows the British Museum to connect with people around the world. The British Museum's website has an entire section devoted to blogs from curators and other staff. These blogs discuss pieces in the museum's collection, conservation projects, and the latest findings from research conducted by museum staff. The British Museum also posts video presentations to the website that provide overviews of past, present, and future exhibits.

In 2013, the British Museum's Mummy: Secrets of the Tomb exhibit opened in Singapore for a six-month stay.

The British Museum sometimes asks outside experts to write blogs about the exhibits as well.

Publications As one of the world's leading museums, the British Museum has a reputation for being an authority on history, archaeology, and conservation. Museum staff share their knowledge of these topics through books and other publications. Some books focus on a specific exhibit, providing photographs and descriptions of the artifacts. Others discuss research projects that have been undertaken by museum staff. While some of these publications are for other **academics**, many are produced for the general public and provide valuable insight into the work the British Museum does.

The British Museum gift shop carries most of the institution's publications.

Education Programs The British Museum has several educational programs that have been tailored to learners of all ages. Special times are set aside for schoolchildren to visit exhibits that relate to their classes. The museum has even created learning kits that teachers can download prior to the visit. The kits prepare students for what they will see when they arrive. The museum also has programs for adults ages 55 and older. Some of these programs take place at the museum, but museum staff will also bring artifacts to seniors groups that cannot visit the museum.

Every year, the British Museum hosts sleepovers for children, allowing them to spend time with their favorite exhibits.

Looking to the Future

The British Museum continues to develop the scope of its collections and its operations. In 2014, the museum opened its World Conservation and Exhibitions Centre. The centre includes state-of-the-art conservation labs and storage facilities, as well as more gallery space. In the coming years, the museum plans to make this centre a hub for learning, conserving, and exhibiting.

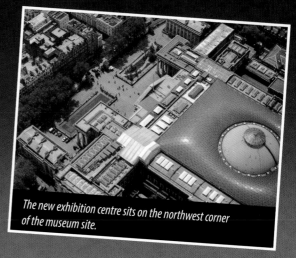

The new exhibition centre sits on the northwest corner of the museum site.

In recent years, the Greek government has challenged the British Museum's ownership of the Parthenon sculptures and has requested their return. The British Museum has declined this request, stating that the sculptures should be part of a collection that focuses on world history. However, the museum continues to cooperate with Greek cultural institutions to gain a better understanding of the artifacts in its care.

People from around the world come to the British Museum to see and study the Parthenon sculptures.

Activity

Many of the British Museum's galleries show artifacts that are unique to specific peoples. Viewing these artifacts fosters an understanding of who these people were, what they cared about, and how they lived. Imagine that you have been asked to create an exhibit for a museum. Your exhibit is to help people get to know you and your family.

Use the guidelines below to plan your exhibit.

1. Think about the items in your home that would tell people the story of your family. These items can include photographs, sports equipment, musical instruments, favorite DVDs, etc. Select 10 items, or artifacts, that you feel best represent your family.

2. Using blank index cards, create a description card for each item. The card should list what the item is, who it belongs to, how long it has been in your family, and why it is important to your collection.

3. Plan the layout of your exhibit. In what order should the works be displayed? Which works should be grouped together? Why?

4. Ask your parents for permission to create an exhibit with your artifacts. Find an open space in your home to display your artifacts. Place the correct description card beside each item.

5. Invite your friends and family into your gallery. Give them a tour of your exhibit. Make sure to explain what your exhibit is about and why each artifact was chosen.

British Museum Quiz

1 How many artifacts are in the British Museum collections?

4 Where were the Lewis Chessmen discovered?

2 What country did the Parthenon sculptures come from?

3 How many curatorial and research departments does the British Museum have?

5 What is the other name for the Easter Island statue?

ANSWERS:

1. More than 8 million **2.** Greece **3.** 10 **4.** On the Isle of Lewis in Scotland **5.** Moai

Key Words

academics: people who study at a university

antiquities: objects from ancient times

artifacts: objects that were made by people in the past

benefactors: financial supporters

botanist: a scientist who studies plants

collection: art and artifacts collected for exhibit and study in a museum, and kept as part of its holdings

conservators: people who protect objects from deterioration

context: the setting of a word or event

cultures: groups of people with shared customs and traditions

curatorial: relating to the management, study, and care of a museum collection

ethnographic: relating to the descriptions of specific cultures

excavated: removed an object by digging

exhibits: displays of objects or artwork within a theme

Grand Tour: a tour of Europe intended to educate young men in the 1700s

humidity: moisture in the air

indigenous: native to a particular place

Industrial Revolution: an economic period in British history that saw the country move from agriculture to industry

medieval: the period of time associated with the 12th to the 15th centuries

patron: a supporter of an institution

Royal Society: a group committed to advancing knowledge of science

solvents: substances in which other substances are dissolved

specimens: animals or plants collected as examples of a particular category

trustees: people appointed to administer the affairs of an institution

Index

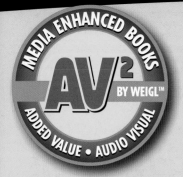

Log on to www.av2books.com

AV² by Weigl brings you media enhanced books that support active learning. Go to www.av2books.com, and enter the special code found on page 2 of this book. You will gain access to enriched and enhanced content that supplements and complements this book. Content includes video, audio, weblinks, quizzes, a slide show, and activities.

AV² Online Navigation

Audio
Listen to sections of the book read aloud.

Book Pages
AV² pages directly correspond to pages in the book.

Video
Watch informative video clips.

Key Words
Study vocabulary, and complete a matching word activity.

Embedded Weblinks
Gain additional information for research.

Try This!
Complete activities and hands-on experiments.

Quizzes
Test your knowledge.

Slide Show
View images and captions, and prepare a presentation.

AV² was built to bridge the gap between print and digital. We encourage you to tell us what you like and what you want to see in the future.

Sign up to be an AV² Ambassador at www.av2books.com/ambassador.